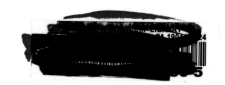

⭐ WOMEN in the U.S. ARMED FORCES ⭐

Women of the U.S. Marine Corps

BREAKING BARRIERS

by Heather E. Schwartz

Consultant:
Nancy Wilt
Women Marines Association Historian
Curator of the Women of the Corps Collection
Castle Rock, Colorado

CAPSTONE PRESS
a capstone imprint

Snap Books are published by Capstone Press,
151 Good Counsel Drive, P.O. Box 669, Mankato, Minnesota 56002.
www.capstonepub.com

Books published by Capstone Press are manufactured with paper
containing at least 10 percent post-consumer waste.

Library of Congress Cataloging-in-Publication Data
Schwartz, Heather E.
 Women of the U.S. Marine Corps : breaking barriers / [Heather E. Schwartz].
  p. cm. — (Snap. Women in the U.S. armed forces)
 Summary: "Describes the past, present, and future of women in the U.S. armed forces"—Provided by publisher.
 ISBN 978-1-4296-5450-0 (library binding)
 1. United States. Marine Corps—Women—Juvenile literature. 2. Women marines—United States—Juvenile literature.
I. Title.
 VE23.S34 2011
 359.9'60820973—dc22   2010033008

Editor: Mari Bolte
Designers: Juliette Peters and Kyle Grenz
Production Specialist: Laura Manthe

Photo Credits:
AP Images, 14, Ed Bailey, 7, Haraz N. Ghanbari, 6, Julie Jacobson, 21; Corbis: Bettmann, 16; DoD photo by Sgt. Evan
Barragan, cover; Getty Images Inc.: AFP/Tim Sloan, 5, Scott Olson, 25; Photo courtesy of The Women of the Corps
Collection, Women Marine Association, 11, 12, 13, 15, 23; Shutterstock: Jason Grower, 9; U.S. Marine Corps photo, 17,
26, Cpl. Erik S. Anderson, 19, Cpl. Erin A. Kirk, 22, Lance Cpl. Paul Miller, 27; U.S. Navy photo, 20

Artistic Effects:
Shutterstock: Maugli

Printed in the United States of America in North Mankato, Minnesota.
092010   005933CGS11

TABLE of CONTENTS

Chapter 1
ANSWERING the CALL 4

Chapter 2
A BIT of HISTORY 10

Chapter 3
The FEW, the PROUD 18

Chapter 4
The FUTURE of WOMEN
in the MARINES 24

Fast Facts 28

Timeline 28

Glossary 30

Read More 31

Internet Sites 31

Index 32

ANSWERING the CALL

Piloting the President

In late 2006, George W. Bush boarded the HMX-1 helicopter known as Marine One. The president came up behind the co-pilot in the helicopter's cockpit. He gave the co-pilot a friendly slap on the shoulder. That's when he got a surprise. The co-pilot was Major Jennifer Grieves. "I think I scared him a little bit when I turned around, and he saw I was a woman," she said.

In May 2008, Jennifer startled the president again. This time, he did a double take. Jennifer was sitting in the pilot's seat. It wasn't that the president doubted her skills. But a woman had never piloted Marine One.

Jennifer drew on her training and trust in the crew to complete her mission. She focused on flying the aircraft. Carrying the president of the United States was simply part of her job as a Marine.

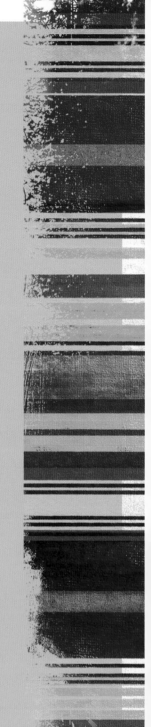

Jennifer Grieves was one of 70 pilots who flew HMX-1 helicopters for the White House.

When Jennifer was growing up, she never imagined she would pilot Marine One. But she did know that she wanted to do something big with her life. Jennifer just didn't know what it would be.

After high school, Jennifer wanted a challenge. Some friends had joined the U.S. Marine Corps. They told her the Marines was the most challenging branch of military service. While those friends were men, Jennifer knew she could make the same choice. She wanted to succeed as a Marine too. At age 19, she joined.

Jennifer Grieves joined the Marine Corps in 1990.

Training gives young Marines the core values of honor, courage, and commitment.

From the start, Jennifer knew she'd made the right decision. "I loved boot camp. I was young and able to do all the things they wanted me to do," she said. "It wasn't fun, but I felt like I matured. It's good to be challenged and feel like you've accomplished something when you're done."

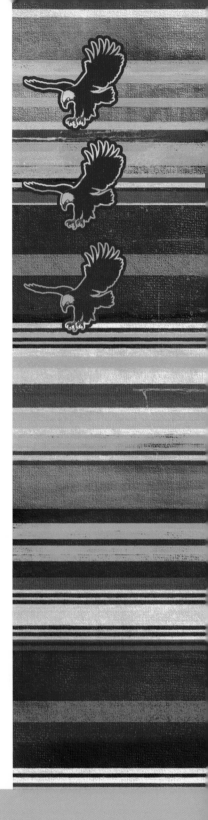

Jennifer enjoyed being part of a Marine unit. Her **platoon** worked together. They grew as close as a family. While on active duty, Jennifer attended the University of Maryland at College Park. Jennifer's advisor encouraged her to take an **aviation** skills test. The test sparked Jennifer's interest in flying.

After college, Jennifer entered the Marine Corps Aviation program in Pensacola, Florida. In the program, she learned to fly three different types of helicopters. She served as a pilot from 2001 to 2005. In 2003 she was **deployed** to Africa during Operation Iraqi Freedom (2003–).

While in Africa, Jennifer's executive officer told her she should apply for the Marine One program. Marine One pilots are trusted to carry the president and other important leaders. They need to get special security clearances, known as Top Secret and Yankee White. Pilots may wait for a year for these clearances.

Marine One pilots are on-call all the time. The HMX-1 helicopters have to be ready to fly anywhere, any time. The pilots must maintain their helicopters and make sure they pass quality inspections.

platoon: a small group of soldiers who work together

aviation: science of building and flying aircraft

deploy: to position troops for combat

Jennifer was accepted to the Marine One program in 2005. While serving as a co-pilot, her passengers included vice presidents and heads of state. She became a Marine One pilot on May 15, 2008.

As a Marine One pilot, Jennifer flew both President George W. Bush and President Barack Obama. Her job took her to seven countries. During her last flight in July 2009, she had an all-female crew. It was another first for the Marines. "It's not really about being a female," Jennifer has said. "It's about being a Marine and about being part of an organization that is exceptional."

HMX-1 helicopters are only known as Marine One when the president is onboard.

CHAPTER 2

A BIT of HISTORY

The "Marinettes"

The Marine Corps was officially formed on November 10, 1775. The Revolutionary War (1775–1783) had just started. Men wanted to fight for their country's independence.

Although women were not allowed into battle, there are stories of women serving their country. Some were spies and learned important information about the enemy's plans. Others followed their husbands to battle. These women cooked meals, washed clothes, and tended wounds. Still others stood by their husbands on the frontlines. And a small few dressed as men and joined the fight.

By the War of 1812 (1812–1815), women disguised themselves as men in order to serve. In those days, men could join the military at a young age. And they were not examined by doctors before joining. Soldiers without facial hair or deep voices were not uncommon. The first woman who claimed to have served as a Marine was Lucy Brewer.

In 1816 a book called *The Female Marine, or The Adventures of Lucy Brewer* was published. Lucy said that she had dressed as a man to serve aboard the USS *Constitution*.

LADY LEATHERNECK

LUCY BREWER YEARNED FOR ADVENTURE – AND FOUND IT BY BECOMING AMERICA'S FIRST LADY LEATHERNECK.

Lucy Brewer has been called the first "Lady Leatherneck."

Lucy, or George Baker as she was known, fought in three major battles. At the end of the war, she returned home to Pennsylvania. For years, people thought the story was a lie. They didn't believe a woman could have done those things. But the book had many details that only a Marine would know. Today many experts view the story as a Marine legend that may someday be proven true.

Opha Mae Johnson (middle) was the first woman to officially join the Marine Corps.

Nearly 140 years later, women were finally allowed to join the Marines. Opha Mae Johnson signed up on August 13, 1918. She served during World War I (1914–1918) with 304 other women.

The new Marines were called "Marinettes." They worked office jobs previously held by male Marines. Their jobs now taken care of, the men were free to serve overseas.

Women worked in public relations, payroll and finance, and at military supply centers. They also took part in daily drills. Some worked guard duty near important buildings in Washington, D.C.

Unlike male Marines, women were not given health care or other veteran's benefits. When the war was over, all women were **discharged** by November 11, 1919.

discharge: to release or dismiss

In 1944 the cosmetics company Elizabeth Arden released a line of makeup that women could wear with their Marine uniforms.

Valuable Recruits

Nearly 25 years later, the world was at war again. Government leaders realized that women were important to the nation's defense. They allowed women to once again enter military service in November 1942. The following spring, the Marine Corps Women's Reserve was established. A call went out for **recruits**. The message was, "Be a Marine ... Free a Marine to Fight!"

More than 20,000 women answered the call. This time they were not limited to office work. Women held more than 200 different jobs. They were mapmakers, mechanics, and aircraft ground crew members. They taught recruits, both male and female, how to use weapons.

recruits: new members to a group

For the first time, women could train to be officers. More than 1,000 women were recruited. They came from colleges and universities throughout the country. Officer candidates needed at least two years of college before applying.

But what would the new Marines be called? The press suggested Femarines, Dainty Devil Dogs, and even Glamarines. In the end, more neutral names were chosen. The United States Marine Corps Women's Reserve was USMCWR. From then on, the new Marines were referred to as WRs or Women Marines. The Marine Corps was the only military branch that gave women and men the same job titles.

Nearly 19,000 female Marines trained at Camp Lejeune in North Carolina during World War II.

During World War II, women performed nearly 90 percent of all Marine operations in the United States.

After World War II ended, most women in the armed services were discharged. Two hundred remained on active duty. They dealt with issues related to the end of the war, including the discharge of other Marines, accounting, and supply.

President Harry S. Truman signed the Women's Armed Services Integration Act on June 12, 1948. This law meant women could hold many military positions previously open only to men. They would not be immediately discharged after serving during a war. They could also get military benefits. Women were finally allowed to serve as full, permanent members of the Marine Corps.

On February 23, 1949, female Marines began their official training. The new recruits reported at Parris Island, South Carolina. They learned Marine history, customs, and courtesy. They learned how to live as Marines.

Female Marines took tests to choose the best military jobs for them. Marching in formation, physical fitness, and being part of a unit were important. But the new Marines also learned the appropriate colors for lipstick and nail polish. There were even rules about what women should wear underneath uniforms. And they did not receive weapons training.

The last lesson was "high tea." Graduates were expected to use proper manners to plan and host the event. During tea, they would make conversation with officers and guests. They were graded on their hairstyles, manners, and conversation skills. It was hoped that these fashionable Marines would encourage other women to join.

In 1945 men marched off to war while women took their place at Marine stations throughout the country.

Men and women in the Marines are held to the same high standards of dress.

While women were not allowed in combat, they continued to serve during wars. Nearly 2,800 female Marines served in the Korean War (1950–1953). About 2,700 female Marines served in the Vietnam War (1959–1975). By 1985 female recruits learned how to fire both rifles and pistols. In 1989 training for **combat** was added.

Today training is the same for both men and women. All recruits fire weapons, crawl through barbed wire, and march in formation. Nobody is a Marinette. Everyone is a Marine.

combat: fighting between people or armies

CHAPTER 3

The FEW, the PROUD

The Making of a Marine

Today Marines spend 13 weeks training at Parris Island. **Basic training** includes physical conditioning, weapons training, and academic classes. Women and men receive the same training. Only their living quarters are separate.

Recruits are immediately put to work. They go through tough physical tests. They learn how to use and fire weapons. They also complete an obstacle course. In the final weeks of boot camp, recruits stage a pretend war. The skills they learn here will help them while in a real combat situation.

The last test recruits must pass is called The Crucible. For 54 hours, recruits work in teams. They solve problems such as how to rescue someone from the top of a building. They get little food or sleep. During a 48-mile (77.2-kilometer) march, the recruits must carry gear weighing more than 45 pounds (20 kilograms). When they finally arrive back at the base, their training is over. They are ready to serve as Marines.

Marines undergoing *The Crucible* must work as both leaders and teammates.

basic training: the first training period for people who join the military

Modern Marines serve their country in many ways. They are electricians, technicians, and mail clerks. They can be gunners, communications specialists, and intelligence officers.

Women have been allowed to take part in air combat since 1993. Today female Marines can serve in nearly any position open to male Marines. To do their jobs, Marines must travel long distances and sometimes through dangerous areas. The battlefield today is huge. If enemies target them on the ground, Marines may have to fight back.

In 1993 Captain Sarah Deal was the first female Marine to start flight training.

Women At War

Between 2001 and 2010, 1,600 female Marines had served multiple **tours** in Afghanistan. About 7,400 more have also served multiple times in Iraq. More than 8,000 female Marines have made a single trip to either of these war zones.

Vernice Armour served in both the Army and the Marines.

In 2002 Captain Vernice Armour became the military's first female African-American combat pilot. She did two combat tours in Iraq. She flew close air support and convoy escorts over enemy areas in AH-1W SuperCobras. "Often we returned to our base in Kuwait with bullet holes in our helicopters," she said.

tour: a set amount of service time

Women Only

In Iraq and Afghanistan, there are some jobs only Marine women can hold. Through the Lioness Program, female Marines search Iraqi women who might be **smuggling** weapons. In some Muslim-populated areas, male Marines cannot perform the search. The job takes female Marines to checkpoints and other places they might not normally be allowed.

Some Marine women work with groups such as the Sisters of Fallujah, a security group made of local Iraqi women.

smuggle: to bring something into or out of a country illegally

Female Marines get to know the local people and earn their trust.

In Afghanistan Muslim women may not talk with men they don't know. But they can speak to women. Female Marines work in Female Engagement Teams. Their mission is to form relationships with Afghan women. The Marines wear headscarves as a sign of respect for the Muslim culture. They meet Afghan women, give them supplies, and gain their trust.

CHAPTER 4

The FUTURE of WOMEN in the MARINES

Reaching Recruits

Not long ago, the Marine Corps sought mainly male recruits. Their slogan in the 1990s called for "a few good men." Ads designed to attract women focused mainly on appearance. These ads encouraged women to "get a makeover that's more than skin deep." They also used tag lines like, "You can look like a model, or you can be one."

Modern efforts to recruit women show how far female Marines have come. Recent ads show women in leadership roles, both for officers and enlisted. These ads stress duty and opportunity to women in the Corps.

More than 13,000 women serve in active duty today. They leave family, friends, and their homes to serve their country. Tours may take them halfway around the world. Female Marines fight hard to be seen as equals to men. Some have even had to convince their families that women belong in the armed forces. But many change their minds when they see their daughters, wives, and sisters becoming Marines.

Female Marines go through basic training at Parris Island, 2007

Female Marines are ready to show they are just as capable as men.

Beyond the Call of Duty

Today female Marines are allowed to fill all but a few combat jobs. Since the 1960s, the roles women have been allowed to play have only increased. Women in the Marine Corps can serve in at least 95 percent of all military positions. In the future, they may be allowed to do any and all jobs asked of them.

The wars in Iraq and Afghanistan have placed women in the line of fire. Both male and female Marines serving in a war may find themselves under fire. If they are being shot at, their main job becomes secondary. In combat, their mission is to defend their country and their fellow Marines.

Today's female Marines are ready to go beyond the call of duty. They work in dangerous conditions. They are trained to use weapons and fight when necessary to defend their country. By performing difficult tasks, they create a future filled with opportunities for women in the Marines.

Women in the Marine Corps go above and beyond their duties while in the line of fire.

FAST FACTS

⭐ About 2,400 female recruits train at Parris Island each year. The average female graduate is 19 years old.

⭐ In November 2000, martial arts training was added to boot camp. Recruits receive 15 hours of training during camp and another six hours during combat training.

⭐ An 18-year-old female Marine must perform 50 crunches in two minutes to pass the physical fitness test.

TIMELINE

June 12
The Women's Armed Services Integration Act gives women full status in the military.

1775   **1918**   **1948**   **1949**

November 10
The U.S. Marine Corps is formed.

August 13
Opha Mae Johnson is the first woman to officially join the Marines.

February 23
Female recruits begin training at Parris Island, South Carolina.

⭐ Currently 6.2 percent of Marines are women.

⭐ The Marine Corps is the only branch of the U.S. armed forces to fight in every American war.

⭐ The motto of the Marines is "Semper Fidelis," or "Always Faithful."

⭐ The unofficial mascot of the Marines is the Devil Dog. The dog is an English bulldog who wears a Marine Corps helmet. It lives in Washington, D.C. In 2006 Molly became the first female bulldog to fill this roll.

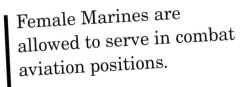

Female Marines are allowed to serve in combat aviation positions.

The Lioness Program is established in Iraq.

1993   **1994**   **2005**   **2009**

The Pentagon prohibits women from serving in certain ground combat positions.

Female Engagement Teams are established in Afghanistan.

GLOSSARY

aviation (ay-vee-AY-shuhn)—science of building and flying aircraft

basic training (BAY-sik TRANE-ing)—the first training period for people who join the military; basic training is sometimes called boot camp

combat (KOM-bat)—fighting between people or armies

deploy (deh-PLOY)—to position troops for combat

discharge (DISS-charj)—to release or dismiss

platoon (pluh-TOON)—a small group of soldiers who work together

recruits (ri-KROOT)—new members to a group

smuggle (SMUHG-uhl)—to bring something in or out of a country illegally

tour (TOOR)—a set amount of service time; also known as tour of duty

READ MORE

David, Jack. *United States Marine Corps.* Torque: Armed Forces. Minneapolis: Bellweather Media, 2008.

Goldish, Meish. *Marine Corps: Civilian to Marine.* Becoming a Soldier. New York: Bearport Publishing, 2011.

Walsh, Francis. *Daring Women of the American Revolution.* American History Flashpoints. New York: Powerkids Press, 2009.

INTERNET SITES

FactHound offers a safe, fun way to find Internet sites related to this book. All of the sites on FactHound have been researched by our staff.

Here's all you do:

Visit *www.facthound.com*

Type in this code: 9781429654500

INDEX

Afghanistan, 21, 22, 23, 27
AH-1W SuperCobras (helicopters), 21
Armour, Vernice, 21
aviation, 8

basic training. *See* boot camp
boot camp, 7, 15, 18
Brewer, Lucy, 10–11
Bush, George W., 4, 9

Camp Lejeune, 14
combat, 17, 18, 20, 21, 26
Crucible, The, 18, 19

Deal, Sarah, 20

Female Engagement Teams, 23

Grieves, Jennifer, 4–9

HMX-1 (helicopter). *See* Marine One.

Iraq, 8, 21, 22, 27

Johnson, Opha Mae, 12

Korean War, 17

Lioness Program, 22

Marine Corps Women's Reserve, 13, 14
Marine One, 4, 6, 8, 9
Marinettes, 12, 17

Obama, Barack, 9
officers, 14, 16, 20
Operation Iraqi Freedom, 8, 21, 22, 27

Parris Island, 18, 25, 28

Revolutionary War, 10

Sisters of Fallujah, 22

Truman, Harry S., 15

United States Marine Corps Women's Reserve (USMCWR), 14

Vietnam War, 17

War of 1812, 10
Women's Armed Services Integration Act, 15
World War I, 12
World War II, 13, 15

ABOUT the AUTHOR

Heather E. Schwartz is the author of several books for Capstone Press. She lives in upstate New York with her husband and young son.